Small Steps To Doing Big Business

Gregory Grant
Justin Stowe

ISBN: 0692125485
ISBN-13: 978-0692125489

DEDICATION

This book is dedicated to all start-up business owners. Our goal is to have a positive impact by providing stellar business advice created from our distinct experiences. There is an entrepreneur inside of everyone. If you have dreams and visions it is evident that you have something within that will change the world in your unique way. This book is designed for you to be successful and make an impact on the world in your own way.

Introduction

Tired of your business not growing? According to small business trends nine out of ten businesses fail during the first year. Do you want to know how to prevent this? Grant Business Solutions has created business tips that will assist you from being one of the nine businesses that fail. The purpose of this book is to make you the one company that succeeds in business beyond the first year. In this publication, you will discover many useful business survival strategies and success tips. You will learn customer acquisition methods and why specific operational protocols are necessary for your business to be successful. After you gain the knowledge from this book you must execute what you learn. Once you execute this knowledge your business will experience success. The principles and proven systems shared in this publication has contributed to success in our companies. We look forward to assisting you with your business success.

CONTENTS

3 Steps to Gain Customers

3 Ways Businesses Can Improve their Client Retention Rate

3 Advantages of Having a Tax Planning Strategy

5 Advantages of Obtaining a 501c3 for your Nonprofit Organization

4 Reasons Your Business Needs Professional Bookkeeping Services

4 Reasons Your Business Needs an Income Producing Website

3 Reasons Why You Must Have A Business Plan

know the Differences Between For-Profit and Non-Profit

Protect Your Intellectual Property by Copyrighting or Trademarking Your Business Idea

The Most Important Pages for Your Small Business Website

Why Your Business Needs an Email List

Why Your Business Must Maintain Professional Financial Records

Why Every Small Business Owner Should be on LinkedIn

ACKNOWLEDGMENTS

The Grant Business Solutions team would like to give a special thanks to everyone that provided inspiration for this publication.

To our Chief Executive Officer, Gregory Grant, for providing expert business leadership to the business community. Many start-up companies and existing businesses have benefited from your expert business solutions. Thank you for sharing your knowledge and being an author of this book.

To our Marketing Consultant, Justin Stowe, for being a co-author of this book. Your viewpoints on business tools used for entrepreneurial success has made a positive impact on many start-up companies. Thank you for sharing.

To our business team, supporters, and clients, we thank you very much for supporting us by reading our publication. Execute these business tips in this book. It will improve your business if you do.

3 STEPS TO GAIN CUSTOMERS

One of the top questions I receive during business consultations is: "How do I get customers to use my services or products?"

I have a simple three-step process to assist business owners with gaining customers. This process is called a customer acquisition strategy. Every business must have one. If you do not have a customer acquisition strategy you are hurting your business growth. The purpose of this strategy is to get people to use your product or service to meet your monthly revenue goals for your company. In 1954, Author and Business Consultant Peter Drucker coined the term SMART goals. The acronym means that all goals should be **S**pecific, **M**easurable, **A**chievable, **R**ealistic, and **T**ime sensitive. The three-step system that I am about to share with you must be aligned to your business goals to experience a successful outcome.

The name of our client acquisition strategy is called the CSQ method. This a proprietary strategy that has been very successful in my entrepreneur journey. CSQ stands for convenience, service, and quality. These are the three steps that must be followed in this specific order. These are among the primary reasons why customers choose to do business with you or your competition. More than ever before major companies are focused on customer innovation using the "convenience factor" as the foundation. According to UX Magazine, there was a study done in 2002 known as the "convenience orientation" which states that a person's preference for convenience has a major impact on purchasing decisions.

Convenience is the way we help our customers reduce their time and effort of buying a product or service. Companies that do this well are experiencing growth. Therefore, as a business owner you must make your products or services very convenient for potential clients. The item or business that has the most "convenience factor" is where customers will be drawn. Make this a priority in your customer acquisition strategy.

Service is how we make our customers feel. Convenience is a tool to get a customer to do business initially, but good customer service provides customer retention. According to a recent article at entrepreneur.com, customer retention is less expensive than customer acquisition. The rationale is that existing customers are more likely to buy from you than a new customer. Good customer service builds consumer trust and confidence in your business. This confidence and trust is then leveraged to create retention. Treat your customers with great respect and exceed their expectations. This is a very valuable initiative that will yield dividends to your organization.

Quality is an expectation for today's well-informed consumer. Customers want to feel that you are giving them the absolute best value for the price charged. The simple definition for quality is the degree of excellence in something. Customers will compare your products or services against a competitor, past or present experience, and to their personal perception. It is very important that you deliver a product or service with excellence. Quality will position your company with a winning competitive edge.

Keep this in mind: Convenience will get the customer in the door to give you a chance. Good customer service will keep the customer coming back to you. Quality delivery will create the confidence that you are an expert in your industry in the mind of the customer.

I hope this was helpful to your business in acquiring and retaining customers. If you have any questions or comments, feel free to respond below. For a consultation or to sign up for our current news and information visit the homepage of our website business-solutionsjax.com

3 WAYS BUSINESSES CAN IMPROVE THEIR CLIENT RETENTION RATE

How much repeat business do you regularly receive? Do your customers come back to you again and again? Or do you find yourself having to constantly reach out to new prospects?

Client retention is something on the mind of every small business owner. It is much easier to keep an existing customer than to find a new one. That is why customer service plays such a large role in companies. Especially because the internet makes it easier than ever for customers to share their experiences.

From our experience, here are a few of the best things you can do to improve your client retention and keep them coming back again and again for your help.

Strategy #1: Get to Know Your Customers
As this article from Inc.com talks about, customers like it when a business treats them individually. Nobody wants to feel like just another cog in a wheel. Your customers want to feel like you really understand their situation and how to fix their problem.

There are a few ways to do that. For example, you can check in with the customer regularly to see how the project is going. Spend several minutes talking to them to get a good feel for their thoughts. If something is not going well and it's within your power to control, tell them you will make it right.

During these check-ins, you can also chat about surface level personal things. Here are a few things to ask about:

-What does the client do for fun?
-Does the client have any family?
-Did they do anything fun this weekend/have fun upcoming weekend plans?
-What part of town do they live in?
-Did they watch the latest big sports game?

Do not spend too much chatting, and you must feel out if the customer wants to talk about these things. But investing these few minutes will help your client feel like you are investing in them, and they will be more likely to stick around.

Strategy #2: Get Their Feedback

I touched on checking in regularly with customers. Simply calling them up and asking how the project is going. That is one type of feedback mentioned in this article on Forbes.com, and it works well.

There are other ways to get feedback from your customers as well. It all depends on your industry, but here are a few ideas.

- **Survey**: In general, people do not like to fill out surveys. If you send your customer a 15-page survey, they'll probably stop halfway through. But if you ask a simple 2-4 question survey, there is a good chance you will get some helpful feedback.

- **Social Media:** See if your client is connected to you on social media. Have they Liked your Facebook page? Do they Like or Reply to anything your company posts? If your client is very active on social media with other brands but not yours, that may indicate something.

- **Sampling Program**: Send your customer a new product and ask for a review in return. What do they like about it? What don't they like? Did it perform as expected?

At the end of the day, there are two reasons to have feedback systems. One is so the customer feels like you are investing in them and really want to help. The second is so you can learn what clients want and adjust your offerings, messaging, etc. to better serve them.

Strategy #3: Proactive, Premium Customer Service

Is your customer service proactive, like they talk about in this article from ClientHeartbeat.com?

Most companies are reactive. They do not help a customer until the customer comes to them with a problem.

Being proactive means *you* take the initiative.

- Communicating long wait times
- Telling them their order is behind schedule
- Getting the word out about a change in service

Most small businesses lose customers because their customer service was lacking. Keep it a top priority in your company, and your client retention will stay high.

Conclusion…

Are you interested in more specific advice on how to retain more clients? Grant Business Solutions can help.

3 ADVANTAGES OF HAVING A TAX PLANNING STRATEGY

As a small business owner, taxes will be the single largest expense of your life. Without a tax planning strategy, you are bound to pay more than necessary. That's why we have put together a few advantages of these strategies to think about for 2018 and beyond.

When to Plan Your Tax Strategy

First, let's talk about when you should put this into place. If you have never created a tax planning strategy, we recommend doing it as soon as possible. This will help you make tax-minded decisions going forward.

According to businessreference.com, many small businesses choose to create their strategy halfway through the tax year. This lets them use the previous six months as an indicator for the remaining six. If their tax planning strategy shows they should do something different to minimize taxes, they have time to make that adjustment.

The Accounting Advantage

One major aspect of tax planning is determining the accounting method you are going to use. There are two types: accrual basis and cash flow basis.

Cash flow basis means income is accounted for once the funds are received. Accrual basis means the income is accounted for once the money is earned, even if the funds were not actually received yet.

This article from Investopedia.com highlights a few differences between the two. The primary advantage of the accrual method is it shows a more accurate view of how your company is doing. The disadvantage is its increased complexity.

Your tax professional can help you navigate between these two options. If you do not have an accountant or tax professional helping you, let Grant Business Solutions know so we can help.

The Inventory Advantage

If you are a business that sells physical products, you have two different ways to account for the value of inventory. One is called first-in, first-out, and the other is last-in, first-out.

An article from accountingtools.com breaks down these two methods well. In general, it comes down to the type of products being sold and the state of the economy. In a time of rising prices, last-in, first-out is used since the most recent products will have the higher costs. In times of deflation or products that lose value quickly, first-in, first-out is often used.

This is an important part of your tax planning strategy because all your assets, including the inventory sitting in your warehouses, are accounted for at tax time. Since you must report this information anyway, it makes sense to use an inventory valuation method that maximizes your after-tax income for the year.

The Retirement Advantage

The primary financial concern for many small business owners is whether they will have enough money to retire later in life. They have often sunk every penny that have into the business and are relying on it to fund their retirement.

During your tax planning strategy, the concept of saving for your retirement should be discussed. With the right vehicles, you can both reduce your tax bill and save for retirement at the same time, which is the best of both worlds. For example, the Simplified Employee Pension Retirement Arrangement (SEP IRA) is a great vehicle for these benefits.

The problem is most small business owners do not realize these types of vehicles exist. That is another area where hiring a CPA or tax professional can help.

Conclusion…

These three reasons are just a few advantages of a tax planning strategy. There are more I did not get a chance to dive into, such as managing business equipment purchases. My goal was not to go over every single reason to have a strategy. Instead, it was to shed light on a few ways a tax planning strategy can help your business maximize net profit.

5 ADVANTAGES OF OBTAINING A 501C3 FOR YOUR NONPROFIT ORGANIZATION

Now that it is tax time, it is a great time of year to understand the advantages of what a 501c3 can do for your nonprofit organization. We will start with a quick introduction on what 501c3 is, and then go into the benefits.

What is 501c3?
Properly written as 501(c) (3,) this is the portion of the IRS tax code that provides tax exemption for nonprofit organizations. Usually these are private foundations, private operating foundations, or public charities.

The tax exemption goes a long way towards helping these organizations accomplish their missions. But there is more to it than that. Here are five advantages you should know.

Advantage #1: Credibility

When you start reaching out to the public for donations, they will be interested in learning more about your organization. They want to make sure their money is going towards the cause, not the director's pocket. This article from IRS.gov phrases it like this: "none of its earnings may inure to any private shareholder or individual."

Being designated as a 501(c)(3) organization offers that reassurance and credibility. They will know you are the real thing and will be more likely to donate and support your cause.

Advantage #2: Donations are Tax Deductible

Tax is the single largest expense for both individuals and for-profit organizations. That means people are constantly trying to find ways to reduce the taxes they pay.

Fortunately for them, donations made to nonprofit organizations (such as 501(c)(3) organizations like yours) are tax deductible. This is a huge incentive for some people, as it creates a win-win. They get to support a cause and reduce their tax bill at the same time.

Advantage #3: Discounted Products and Services

Usually a 501(c)(3) organization can negotiate discounts on the products and services they purchase. Businesses like selling to nonprofits at a discount because they feel like they're helping your cause indirectly, while still getting paid for what they offer.

A good example is media outlets. Talk to your local radio stations, TV stations and newspapers. Keep them in the loop with all the great work your organization is doing. They love to hear about how 501(c)(3)s are benefiting the community and can help you get the word out.

Discounts aren't only limited to for-profit businesses though. Government entities may give you discounted rates as well. For example, the U.S. Postal Service may allow you to ship with bulk mailing rates. This is one of the advantages posted on the official 501c3 site.

Advantage #4: Access to Government Grants

Each year, the federal government gives out a lot of money to well-deserving nonprofit organizations. The best source to use is Grants.gov, which is the hub to learn about grants, search for those relevant to you, and more.

Simply by claiming 501(c)(3) status, you open the door to a lot of grants. That does not necessarily mean you will be awarded the grant, but at least it gives you the opportunity to explore these options.

Advantage #5: Tax Exemption

Last but certainly not least is the tax exemption. A 501(c)(3) is exempt from paying federal taxes, and some states offer the same benefit.

As mentioned earlier, taxes are usually the single largest expense for people and organizations. By not having to pay 20-40% of its net earnings, your nonprofit will be able to funnel a lot more money back into accomplishing its mission.

Conclusion…

If your organization is a nonprofit, consider applying for 501(c)(3) status. The advantages are great and can help you both attract donations and save a lot of money over the long run.

4 REASONS YOUR BUSINESS NEEDS PROFESSIONAL BOOKKEEPING SERVICES

Small business owners typically do it all. They are the cook, chef and bottle washer. From marketing to accounting, they must stay on top of every part of the business.

But this is not sustainable.

Once the business gets rolling, the first thing the entrepreneur should outsource is bookkeeping. Here are four reasons why.

Reason #1: Accounting is Complex
There's a reason there is a specific, widely-respected certification for accountants. The work they do is tough and complex.

Sure, you may be able to get away with QuickBooks by yourself when the company first launches. But as this article from foxbusiness.com points out, you will eventually find yourself dealing with increasingly difficult transaction situations.

Here are just a few transactions to manage regularly:

- -Payroll
- -Processing credit cards
- -Buying new equipment
- -Insurance
- -Employee benefits
- -Taxes

That is not even getting into financial statements such as your balance sheet. These are just the daily transactions you need to track. It gets to be a lot, so pay someone else to do it!

Reason #2: It Lets Your Team Focus on Growing the Business

Nobody else cares about growing the business as much as you. That is why you need to stay at the helm and keep driving the business forward, rather than get stuck in the weeds of bookkeeping.

Every hour you spend crunching numbers is an hour you could have spent cold-calling or emailing prospects. It is an hour you could have spent trying a new marketing method, such as Facebook ads. Or working with existing customers to solicit more business from them.

Do you have a small team? That is great- but it still probably does not make sense to keep bookkeeping in-house. Unless someone on your team has bookkeeping experience and some bandwidth to spare, it is better to let someone else focus on it.

Your team member probably already has multiple roles on their plate. They are helping grow the business and take care of customers. That leaves little room to dive into the books. Instead, hire a professional bookkeeping service so your team can focus on growth.

Reason #3: Maximize Your Deductions

Cash is king for small businesses. A penny saved is a penny earned, so maximizing your business deductions on taxes should be a major focus at tax time.

If you are not a certified accountant, you will not know how to get every deduction possible. Sure, you may be able to find some through a software program. But it takes an expert to ensure you are getting credit for every deduction out there.

As this article from bizjournals.com highlights, it is easy for small business owners to overlook certain things. Instead of worrying about it, pay someone else who can focus on it. It is worth the investment both financially and mentally.

Reason #4: The World is Watching

At some point, you will probably want money from an outside entity.

It might be the taxman, your bank, or a group of investors. It does not matter. Outside entities looking at your business are professionals. They know amateur bookkeeping when they see it. Even though it may not completely scare them away, they certainly won't be impressed.

Do not risk your ability to obtain that critical business loan. If you are trying to be acquired, do not be in the position of having poorly kept books make investors look another way.

Instead, spend a few bucks to get your ducks in a row. Your business and your wallet will thank you later.

Conclusion…

These are just a few reasons to invest in a professional bookkeeping services. Note that we didn't even talk about the obvious reasons, like protecting you from a tax audit or helping you avoid wasteful spending.

When you are ready to invest your energy towards growing your business rather than your bookkeeping, let us know. Our professional bookkeeping services will take great care of you.

4 REASONS YOUR BUSINESS NEEDS AN INCOME PRODUCING WEBSITE

"My business is doing just fine without a website."

I'm surprised how many people still say this in 2017. Ten years ago, I could understand. But if you don't have any kind of website right now, you are losing money every day.

There are dozens of reasons why your business needs its own website. But for the sake of your valuable time, I'm going to boil it down to just four reasons.

Reason #1: You Own the Key
Some businesses do very well on social media. They have a Facebook page, lots of Instagram followers, and are active on Twitter.

That is great, but the problem is they do not control those mediums.

Thousands of small business owners have been hurt by relying too much on these platforms. As this great article from GoDaddy points out, If you do something wrong (or even if you do not,) the social media site can delete your account and everything you have built.

Gone.

Even if you do get it back, there was an opportunity cost from not making sales during the downtime, and your customers may have lost some trust in you.

With your own website, that can't happen. You own the content. You own the logo. You own the domain name. You hold the key.

Reason #2: Customers Expect It

How do you feel about a company if you can't find them online?

Do you think "oh that is no big deal?"

Or do you think to yourself "wow, I cannot believe they do not have a site! How am I supposed to learn more about them? Are they legit?"

If you're like 95% of people, it's the latter.

Customers expect a website. They want to do a quick Google search and learn more about you before they buy. That's why the About page is one of the most trafficked pages on business sites.

This is the number one reason Constant Contact gives on why you need a website. If you don't have a site, your customer will just go to your competitors that do have sites.

Customer lost…

Reason #3: Your Website is a 24/7 Salesperson
Even entrepreneurs need to get a little sleep.

But your website does not. Your website is selling for you all the time. It generates business passively once you have it built and traffic coming in.

It does not matter what kind of business you have, either.

Local service business? Customers like to find you online and check out your website before calling. In fact, your website is where they get your phone number!

Sell physical products? Customers expect a website to learn more about the products.

Are you a Software as a Service company? You need a website to help explain your offering.

And since people are shopping around all day long, you need a resource available all-day long.

Reason #4: Design Styles and Technologies Change
This last one is focused more on companies that already have websites.

You would be surprised how many times I'm told "I'm okay, I already have a website."

Yes, that's true. It also looks like it was designed in 1997 with a potato.

Times change. Technologies change.

Most people use the internet with mobile devices more than desktop or laptop computers.

Customers expect a clean site without ugly flash banners.

As the times change, your website needs to change too.

Conclusion…

If you want to build a business that lasts, you need a website in today's marketplace.

Are you ready to have a professional, income-generating website for your business? Or if you already have a site, do you need a redesign?

If you said yes to either of these questions, give us a call. We would love to help you through this process, so you can do what you do best- build your business.

3 REASONS WHY YOU MUST HAVE A BUSINESS PLAN

Creating a business plan is one of the most important things you can do for your business. Whether you plan on keeping it small or want to become the next Amazon, laying out a solid business plan early is critical, as it is the foundation for everything.

There are three reasons why I say that.

Reason #1: Business Plans Identify Strengths and Weaknesses

The marketplace is competitive. To stand out, you need to know what to communicate. For most businesses, that means leveraging strengths and accounting for weaknesses.

According to the Wall Street Journal, this helps you create a realistic snapshot of success. It allows you to reduce the risks of issues caused by your weaknesses.

For example, maybe you are terrific at product creation and operations but terrible at marketing and sales.

Knowing this information, you may decide to hire someone to fill that gap, so you can focus on what you do best.

Another example is maybe you are great at marketing and sales but are lost when it comes to accounting. In that case, you know that hiring a bookkeeper is probably worth considering.

Reason #2: Business Plans Help You Focus

A lot of business owners will tell you they had to pivot at one point or another. They started the business with the intention of selling A, but ended up selling C instead. As it turned out, A and B were not really what the market wanted!

That said, business plans are important because they help you stay focused on one thing at a time. They outline your key strategy. Once the strategy is in place and solidified, tactics are aligned with the strategy to meet your goals.

This article from Entrepreneur.com has a few great examples of what this looks like in real life:

- Your managers will filter everything that happens through the plan as they go about their day.
- Need to hire someone, or buy new equipment? Look at the plan to see if it aligns with the company's vision.
- How the marketing and sales teams work will be largely based on the plan to help improve the brand's identity in the marketplace.

Without a plan, a business becomes more disjointed. Think of the plan as a hub that everything else stems from.

Reason #3: Raising Capital

It is difficult for most businesses to grow past a certain

point without capital investments. As they say, it takes money to make money.

When you go to a bank for an investment in your business, they are going to look for certain things. I love how the Small Business Association puts it: "they (banks) are looking for stability, reliability and responsibility."

In other words, banks want to see a track record. Before they're willing to invest their hard-working money into a business, they want to ensure they are choosing the right horse to back. Financials are an important part of that. But so is showing them your business plan on how you will get from A to B, including how you will overcome obstacles along the way.

Do not think you will ever have to take out capital? Hopefully you are right. But when you reach a point where you could really use another employee or two but do not have the cash flow to hire them, you will be wishing you could go to a bank and ask for the money to grow.

KNOW THE DIFFERENCES BETWEEN FOR-PROFIT AND NON-PROFIT

There are a few misconceptions out there on the differences between non-profit and for-profit organization structures. This article will clear up a few of these misconceptions and give you a better feel for each.

A for-profit organization is designed to funnel profits to the owner and shareholders. In other words, you can just call it a business.

Non-profit organizations are a bit different. They (usually) exist to support society in one way or another. Some support government functions. Others cater to helping people with disabilities find jobs or feed the homeless. Churches and religious organizations are usually non-profits.

As this article from smallbusiness.chron.com puts it, the business differences in these organizations stem from the reason why they exist.

Knowing that, you understand why an entrepreneur

cannot consider their business a non-profit just because they have not made a profit yet! You would be surprised how many small business owners have wondered about that.

How They Make Money

Businesses bring money into the organization through sales of a service or product. There may be investment or credit from outside sources, but the regular cash flow is coming from sales.

Non-profit organizations usually receive money in the form of donations and grants. But as this great article from bplans.com highlights, many non-profits also generate revenue. If this money is generated to help support the mission, it is not taxed.

For example, Mister Migs is a non-profit that helps support its mission by selling handmade dog clothing. They teach work skills to people with disabilities by helping them learn how to create the dog clothing. The clothing is then sold to help support the real mission.

Accounting Differences

One of the biggest differences between these two structures is financial accounting.

For-profit organizations usually have a balance sheet to track assets and expenses. As part of that, the owner's equity in the company is listed as an asset.

Non-profit organizations do not have owners. That means owner's equity does not exist, so they do not use a balance sheet. Instead they file a "statement of financial position" that gives a snapshot of the organization's finances.

Which One is Better?

The answer is - it depends.

If you are an entrepreneur who wants to do very well for yourself financially, a for-profit organization is your best bet. Every sale, every activity helps support you financially. Obviously, you are filling a need in the marketplace, but your overall mission is not focused on benefiting society in the same way a non-profit would.

The best thing about a for-profit organization is the owner can do what they want with the profits. A non-profit can't do that. As this article from Entrepreneur.com points out, non-profits must funnel profits back into the organization once bills are paid.

A non-profit is a better choice if there is a certain social issue you're trying to solve. Maybe you want to help find homes for stray animals. Or help clean up the environment. Whatever your social goal is, a non-profit is probably the best structure for you.

Non-profits have a lot of advantages over for-profits. This article from Forbes, written by the CEO of Common Lit, talks to several reasons why a non-profit is a great structure. One example is the discounts Common Lit often receives on products and services. Another is it's not difficult to receive help from professionals looking to give back to society.

Conclusion…

When you are starting an organization, ask yourself one question: Is this to make me money, or solve a social need? This will help you determine what kind of organization to start.

PROTECT YOUR INTELLECTUAL PROPERTY BY COPYRIGHTING OR TRADEMARKING YOUR BUSINESS IDEA

Two of the best ways to protect your business are trademarks and copyrights. Even though they are not necessary to operate a business, there is no reason not to go through the legal process if you are in business for the long haul.

To illustrate why, let us dive into each of these two entities. First, the trademark.

What is a Trademark?
To summarize USPTO.gov, a trademark is a name that helps distinguish one product or service from the rest in its industry.

You can trademark a brand name, word, symbol, device, or a combination of the above. A good idea if you plan on using a combination is to trademark each individually, as well as the combination itself.

Note that the same word may be trademarked in different industries. For example, a movie company may trademark the word "Termite Terminator," but a pest control company may be able to trademark the same name. That is because they are different industries and do not directly compete.

How Does a Trademark Protect My Business?
Let's stick with the example above. You own a pest control company, and you really want to call one of your services "Termite Terminator." If you do not trademark that phrase, your competition can just copy your service name. In fact, even if you come up with the name and use it first but do not file a trademark before they do, they may end up with the name!

In other words, filing for a trademark will help you ensure the word or phrase remains yours, and yours alone. This will help you stand out in the market, since no other company could copy you directly.

Still not convinced? Keep in mind that you can trademark a company name. Therefore, if unless you are okay with the idea of a competitor copying your name, file a trademark for it!

What is a Copyright?
A copyright is a legal entity that still protects your business but is a bit different. It restricts other parties from being able to use whatever you copyrighted without your consent.

Usually these are used on pieces of art such as written articles, books, music, videos, photographs or images.

How Can a Copyright Protect My Business?
Let us pretend you are spending a lot of time and

energy focusing on drawing customers to your website from the search engines. In other words, you are working on Search Engine Optimization (SEO.)

To rank high in the search engines, you need a lot of content. The problem is if you do not copyright this content, someone can steal (literally just copy-paste) it. To protect it, you can copyright your website. Even though there's a chance someone will still steal your content, you now have the right to take legal action against them if your content was copyrighted.

Or maybe you have a photography business. It is common for photographers to post photos to the public to display their portfolio. If you do not copyright those images, someone can steal them from under your nose.

Conclusion…

You do not need to file for a trademark or copyright to have a sustainable business. But if you want to protect the names and content your business creates, it is a great idea to go through these legal actions.

THE MOST IMPORTANT PAGES FOR YOUR SMALL BUSINESS WEBSITE

What are the most important pages for your small business website? After all, you already know your business needs a website. Now it is just a matter of getting the content put together.

Luckily, you only need to focus on a few pages to start. When you figure the build out of your site, make sure it includes these five pages.

Important Page #1: Home Page

There is a reason why Neil Patel lists this first in this post on HubSpot's blog. This is the hub of your website. Every other piece, from blog posts to products and services, should be easily found on the Home Page.

To get the most out of your Home Page, you just need to ask yourself two questions:

1) What is the visitor looking for?
2) What is your business goal for the visitor?

The first question focuses on understanding your prospect:

- What do they care about?
- How did they get to your site?
- Why are they on your site?

You cannot turn someone into a customer if you do not know them.

The second question relates to getting the visitor to take action. Do you want them to buy something? Sign up for your email list? Whatever it is, you need to set up a Home Page that encourages your visitor to take action.

Important Page #2: About Page

A lot of businesses neglect their about pages. As this post from OpenVine.com highlights, that can be a big mistake. Many your website visitors will check out this page.

There are a few things they may be looking for:

- Learn more about what your business does
- Determine if your business serves their area
- Make sure your business isn't a scam
- Analyze the success of your business

Think of the business-client relationship like dating. When you first start dating someone, you get to know them better. This comes from talking. Asking questions. Learning about each other.

Your business is the same way. Your About Page allows you to tell people what your business is all about. 24 hours a day, seven days a week.

Important Note: Your About Page isn't about how you like to spend your spare time birding or watching movies from the 80s. You can share personal information, but the primary focus is to explain why you (and your business) are best-suited to solve the problems of your visitors.

Important Page #3: Contact Us

You should make it easy for customers to get in touch with you. As this article from Digital.com points out, that means offering numerous touch points.

- Your email address
- A phone number
- A physical mailing address
- P.O. Box
- A Facebook page.

This does not mean you need to provide 20 different options. It is difficult to keep up with too many social media pages. The sweet spot is 2 - 4 different methods. That helps ensure your prospect will reach out, rather than click away from your page.

Important Pages #4 and 5: Privacy Policy and Terms and Conditions…

I have grouped these for a reason. These are not the most exciting pages on your site, but they are important. They tell your visitors what you will do with the personal information they give you and the terms they agree to by visiting your site.

Think of these pages like your website's digital lawyer. They help keep you out of trouble.

Conclusion…

Do you have all these pages for your website? If not, do you need new content to fill those pages?

WHY YOUR BUSINESS NEEDS AN EMAIL LIST

Which is easier - to get a new customer or keep a previous customer coming back?

Any business owner will tell you it is the latter. Acquiring new customers is expensive and time consuming. Successful businesses are built by taking care of their customers and having them come back again and again.

That is why building an email list of both customers and leads is critical. To be more specific, here are a few reasons why your business - no matter what you sell - needs an email list.

Strengthen Relationships…

How do you get to know someone? The short answer is you need to talk to them. Spend time with them.

As this article from Constant Contact points out, email

marketing allows you to do that for hundreds, thousands, or even tens of thousands of people. Even though it is different than talking face to face or on the phone, it is still a way of communicating. You are still building a relationship.

This relationship is important because it helps them get to know you. As they do, they will start to know, like, and trust you. Leads become customers with businesses they know, like, and trust.

Over time, customers may get to a point where they don't even read your sales page or product description. They just buy whatever you put into the market because they know they like you and what you do for them.

Stay Top of Mind…

An article I recently read on ReachLocal.com talked about several ways to stay top of mind with customers. One of those ways is through email marketing.

Most people open their email at least once or twice a day. A lot of us keep it open all day and open every single email as it comes through.

By emailing people at least once a week, you're leveraging those behaviors we've adopted over time. This keeps your customers thinking about you throughout the year.

So, when you announce that new product or service, they may not really need it. By regularly emailing them, they will not forget about you. When they suddenly have a need for what you have to offer, they will go straight to you first.

Start a Conversation…

Earlier, I talked about how email marketing helps your subscribers get to know you. But that was more focused on a one-way communication between you and them.

Something else to keep in mind, as this article from Nectafy points out, is email marketing creates conversations.

For example, let us say you want to do a little market research. At the end of your email, you include a great question that gets dozens of responses from your subscribers.

Now a conversation has started. You asked them something and they took the time to reply. That makes them a great lead to either

1) Keep learning about the issue, or
2) Make a sale

Your customers do not want to just be talked to. They want to be engaged. Email marketing makes that happen.

Test Offers…

Email marketing can help with another aspect of your market research. Instead of asking questions, you can learn about your subscribers through A/B testing.

A/B testing is where you send one email to half of your subscribers and another similar (but not exactly the same) email to the other half.

You can determine the audience preference based on response. If one email gets 100 clicks and the other gets 20, you know which one your audience preferred.

This can be used to test anything from headlines to new product offerings.

Conclusion…

There are dozens of ways you can benefit your small business by building an email list. If you don't invest the time and money, we can almost guarantee you are losing sales.

WHY YOUR BUSINESS MUST MAINTAIN PROFESSIONAL FINANCIAL RECORDS

How does your business maintain financial records? Are they generated using accounting software and stored in the cloud? Are they done simply using Microsoft Excel and kept on your local computer? Do you have a lot of paper documents stored in a filing cabinet?

The method you choose is important, but there is one thing even more important: ensuring your financial records are professional and accurate. There are three main reasons why I say that.

Preparing Financial Statements…

Every small business needs to create financial statements. As this article from the IRS mentions, these statements help you manage your business and deal with banks, creditors and the IRS. .

To create your financial statements, it helps to keep everything well-organized. Here are a few things you'll need:

- Gross Receipts
- Expenses
- Cost of Goods Sold
- Travel, Transportation and Gift Expenses
- Assets
- Employment Taxes

Within each of these, you'll have different forms of documentation. For example, some of your office supplies may be purchased at a local store, where you get a paper receipt. If you pay for online services, you very rarely will get a paper receipt, so instead you will need to record an invoice or other electronic record of payment.

At the end of the day, it does not matter if they are electronic or paper. It just matters that you have them professionally maintained so they can be easily used for generating financial statements.

Filing Your Taxes…

Another reason to maintain professional financial records is for tax purposes. Even though it is just one short sentence in this short guide from the SBA.gov, it is important for protecting yourself.

If your business is not managing its taxes correctly, it may come back to haunt you later. It is not uncommon for a business to get a large bill from the IRS saying they owe back taxes.

A good example is something that happened to a good friend of mine who operates a business across the state of Alabama. For several years, he was sure to pay his taxes and do what he needed to do. But one year he got a huge tax bill, saying he should've been paying taxes to each county he operated in, whereas he had only been paying the county where his office resides.

When you keep your financial records correctly and work with an expert, you are less likely to get into these kinds of situations with your taxes.

Saving Time So You Can Work on Your Business

The most important reason to keep professional financial records does not have anything to do with outside parties.

Sure, your taxes and financial statements are important. But what is more important?

Your business...

This short article from NIBusinessInfo alludes to the fact that saving time is important. As a business owner, you have a lot on your shoulders.

- Keep current customers happy
- Find new customers
- Generate enough sales to pay your employees
- Provide for yourself and your family
- Cut costs without cutting quality

There is always something to be done.

If you are spending a lot of time on financial records, that is a waste of your time. Even though they do require some time, they should not become a burden. Having them maintained the right way, by a professional, will prevent you from wasting time and effort.

Conclusion…

How do you maintain your financial records? Are you still using internal resources that can be better spent on other parts of your business? If so, we would love to help. Here at Grant Business Solutions, we specialize in helping small business with their financial records.

WHY EVERY SMALL BUSINESS OWNER SHOULD BE ON LINKEDIN

If you own a small business, you should be on LinkedIn.

Granted, some businesses will benefit more than others. If you are a business-to-consumer company, how you use it will be different than B2B. The owner of a small coffee shop will use it very differently than the owner of an accounting firm.

No matter what line of work you are in, here are the two main ways you can use this platform: networking and advertising.

Networking…

The main reason you should be on LinkedIn is to leverage its networking power. According to The Balance, just being on LinkedIn opens up doors because you never know when a connection may pass on a business referral. Lewis Howes, a successful entrepreneur, built his business by reaching out to people on LinkedIn.

An entire book can (and has) been written on how to use LinkedIn for networking. For simplicity sake, here are a few best practices.

Introduce yourself - if you reach out to connect with someone, include a short message. Introduce yourself, explain how you found them, and why you want to connect. This is very easy, but most people do not do it. If you do, you will stand out (in a good way.)

Find commonalities - try to find a way you are connected to the person. Did you go to the same college? High school? Have a mutual connection? Leverage that connection to help you build the relationship.

It's not a dating site - unfortunately, a lot of people treat LinkedIn like a dating site. When you reach out to connect with someone, do not make any reference to them being physically attractive or ask them out on a date. Coffee to discuss business is fine - dinner or drinks are not!

As your network grows and you become connected to more people, you may find new opportunities come up. Joint ventures, new employees, business partners, customer, etc.

Networking through Groups…

LinkedIn offers groups in just about every industry you can imagine. Look around and join a few that are relevant to yours. As this article from MarketingThink.com mentions, it is best to join groups that have (at least some) people that live close to you.

The main reason groups can be so useful is the messaging function. LinkedIn only lets you send messages to two types of people: connections and people in the same group as you.

By joining a group, you essentially add hundreds (or thousands) of connections. Even though you will not have a relationship with them right off the bat, you can build that over time.

The best way to do that is to post in the group. Write your own original posts and comment on posts from other people. Everyone loves interaction on social media, so interact!

Advertising…

LinkedIn's pay per click advertising platform has come a long way. Businesses love it because it allows you to market to niche audiences.

For example, let us say you own a small marketing agency, and your clients are usually either brand managers or marketing managers. You can use LinkedIn to target people with those job titles.

This means two things:
1) You are only spending money to get in front of your target market
2) You are increasing awareness and exposure to your brand

Even if someone does not become a customer right now does not mean the money was wasted. They may introduce you to someone who can use your services or decide to work with you at a later time.

Conclusion…

If you own a small business, LinkedIn is a great place to build your network and advertise your company's products and services.

GRANT BUSINESS SOLUTIONS

Grant Business Solutions is a one stop business solutions center that provides resource capital to business owners and management teams. Our company consist of industry experts that assist organizations on how to leverage key resources that generate successful business operations. We work with large and small companies assisting with funding, book-keeping, taxes, business formations, accounting, grant-writing, business plans, branding, marketing, business grants, and much more. As we leverage our experience in these critical areas, business owners and management teams now have more time to focus on growing their businesses. Starting a business and operating a business can be very challenging. We are here to help you minimize those challenges.

www.ingramcontent.com/pod-product-compliance
Lightning Source LLC
Chambersburg PA
CBHW071125210326
41519CB00020B/6420
* 9 7 8 0 6 9 2 1 2 5 4 8 9 *